A Panda's World

written and illustrated by Caroline Arnold

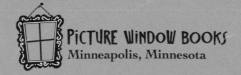

PICTURE WINDOW BOOKS
Minneapolis, Minnesota

Special thanks to our advisers for their expertise:

Zoological Society of San Diego
San Diego Zoo
San Diego, California

Susan Kesselring, M.A., Literacy Educator
Rosemount–Apple Valley–Eagan (Minnesota) School District

Editor: Christianne Jones
Designer: Nathan Gassman
Page Production: James Mackey
Creative Director: Keith Griffin
Editorial Director: Carol Jones
The illustrations in this book were created with cut paper.

Picture Window Books
5115 Excelsior Boulevard
Suite 232
Minneapolis, MN 55416
877-845-8392
www.picturewindowbooks.com

Printed in the United States of America.

Library of Congress Cataloging-in-Publication Data
Arnold, Caroline.
A panda's world / written and illustrated by Caroline Arnold.
p. cm. — (Caroline Arnold's animals)
Includes bibliographical references and index.
ISBN 1-4048-1322-5 (hard cover)
1. Giant panda—Juvenile literature. I. Title.

QL737.C214A76 2005
599.789—dc22   2005023162

Giant Pandas

Where they live: China

Habitat: mountain forests

Food: bamboo

Length: 6 feet (1.8 meters)

Weight: 250 to 300 pounds (113 to 135 kilograms)

Animal class: mammals

Scientific name: *Ailuropoda melanoleuca*

A panda baby is called a cub. Follow a giant panda cub as he grows up in China and learn about a panda's world.

High in the mountains of China, a giant panda walks through a forest. Her four padded feet crunch the dry leaves. Her two round ears listen for danger.

The panda stops and sniffs the cool, damp air. Winter is coming. It is time to go to her den. Her baby will be born soon.

When a female is ready to give birth, she looks for a hollow tree or dry cave to use as a den.

The mother panda curls up inside her den. She holds her new baby in her paw. His tiny pink body is covered with fine, white hair. His eyes are shut tight.

The baby panda squeals. He is hungry. His mother holds him close so he can drink some milk.

A newborn panda weighs about 4 ounces (112 grams). It is no bigger than a stick of butter.

The baby panda grows quickly. By the time he is six weeks old, he has soft, black and white fur all over his tiny body. He looks like a living teddy bear.

The mother panda has not had much to eat since her baby was born. She picks up the baby panda and tucks him safely in a corner of the den. Then she goes out to look for food.

At six weeks, a baby panda weighs about 6 pounds (2.7 kg). His eyes are beginning to open.

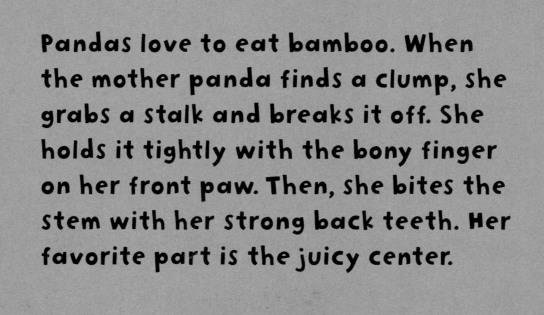

Pandas love to eat bamboo. When the mother panda finds a clump, she grabs a stalk and breaks it off. She holds it tightly with the bony finger on her front paw. Then, she bites the stem with her strong back teeth. Her favorite part is the juicy center.

A full grown panda can eat up to 40 pounds (18 kg) of bamboo a day.

squirrel

The baby panda is now three months old.
He can walk a few steps by himself.
While his mother is away
looking for food, he
creeps to the front
of the den.

A three-month-old panda
weighs about 13 pounds
(6 kg).

takin

He watches a squirrel scamper in the branches above. He sees two takin munching on grass at the edge of the clearing. Nearby, a golden pheasant pecks for seeds. The panda makes a sound, and the pheasant darts away.

golden pheasant

13

The baby panda is now six months old. He follows his mother through the forest. When they find some bamboo, he nibbles the leaves.

14

One day, a leopard tries to catch the pandas by surprise. Mother panda growls and scares it away.

leopard

A six-month-old panda has 24 baby teeth. These will gradually be replaced with a set of 42 adult teeth.

The young panda hears a noise. He scrambles up a tree. Five sharp claws on each paw help him hold on tightly.

Pandas are good climbers. This helps keep them safe from leopards and other predators on the ground.

golden monkeys

The panda peers through the branches. He sees some chattering monkeys. That's where all that noise is coming from! He finds a fork in the tree and lays down to rest.

The young panda has his first birthday. Soon, the days grow cold. Snow flutters to the ground. The young panda and his mother don't mind. Their thick fur keeps them warm and dry.

When the weather is stormy, the pandas find shelter. After the storm passes, they go out again and look for food under the snow.

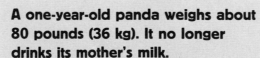

A one-year-old panda weighs about 80 pounds (36 kg). It no longer drinks its mother's milk.

Spring comes and the snow melts. Flowers poke up from beneath the ground. The young panda is now a year and a half old. His mother leaves to look for a mate. She will not come back.

Now the young panda must find his own food.
He must watch out for danger by himself.
He is big enough to be on his own. The young
panda will continue to grow and will find his
own mate one day.

Where do pandas live?

Giant pandas live in the Sichuan, Gansu, and Shaanxi provinces of China. The cool, wet climate is perfect for growing the bamboo that pandas need to eat. More than 40 inches (102 centimeters) of rain and snow fall each year. This moisture keeps the forest wet.

CHINA

PACIFIC OCEAN

the yellow part of the map represents where pandas live

PANDA FUN FACTS

Grass Eating Bears

Up to 99 percent of a panda's diet is bamboo. Bamboo is a type of grass. Its tall stalks can grow to the size of small trees.

Panda Perfume

Pandas have a good sense of smell. A male panda can find a female by her scent.

Gifts of Friendship

The first panda to leave China was brought to the United States in 1936 by an American explorer named Ruth Harkness. She took her young panda, named Su-Lin, to New York and Chicago. The pandas that live outside of China today are gifts of friendship from China. You can see giant pandas in many zoos around the world.

Panda Life

Pandas do not usually live more than 20 years in the wild. They can live more than 30 years at zoos. The oldest panda lived for 37 years.

Endangered Animals

Pandas are in danger of becoming extinct. About 1,600 giant pandas live in the wild. People are working to protect them and help them find all the things they need to survive.

Glossary

bamboo—*a tall, stick-like plant with hard, hollow stems*

clearing—*open land in the middle of a forest*

climate—*average weather of a place throughout the year*

habitat—*the place and natural conditions in which a plant or an animal lives*

mammals—*warm-blooded animals that feed their babies milk*

mate—*the male or female of a pair of animals*

pheasant—*a large bird with a long tail*

predators—*animals that hunt and eat other animals*

stalk—*main stem or part of a plant*

takin—*a large animal related to the musk ox and mountain goat*

To Learn More

At the Library

Bredeson, Carmen. *Giant Pandas Up Close*. Berkeley Heights, N.J.: Enslow Publishers, 2006.

Cooper, Jason. *Cub to Panda*. Vero Beach, Fla.: Rourke Pub., 2004.

Levine, Michelle. *Giant Pandas*. Minneapolis: Lerner Publications, 2006.

On the Web

FactHound offers a safe, fun way to find Internet sites related to this book. All of the sites on FactHound have been researched by our staff.

1. Visit *www.facthound.com*

2. Type in this special code for age-appropriate sites: 1404813225

3. Click on the FETCH IT button.

Your trusty FactHound will fetch the best sites for you!

Index

Look for all of the books in the Caroline Arnold's Animals series: